Age of Adolescence

MaryAnn Hayatian

© 2019 Maryann Hayatian
ButterflyAnthology
ISBN 978-1-989277-02-7
All rights reserved. No part of this book may be reproduced, stored in a
retrieval system or transmitted in any form or by any means without the prior
written permission of the publishers, except by a reviewer who may quote
brief passages in a review to be printed in a newspaper, magazine or journal

ButterflyAnthology

www.butterflyanthology.com

Family

thank you for giving

support I needed

when I aspired to have my accomplishments
completed
Dad
thanks for being proud
and believing in me for the
skills I've gained today
You will always be missed

Poetry:
Art
or
work
of a poet

Never be afraid to be a dreamer
you will find the path to your successful journey
Mia

Poetry

Age of Adolescence 11,12

Like a Runaway 13, 14

Attic 15

The Waiting Game 16,17

Waiting for Liberty 18,19

Describes You 20

One Summer Day 21

Another Storm 22

A Part of Reality 23

Why? I Think 24

Wish 25

My Heart is Bloomed 26

Midsummer's Day 27

You're Always There 28

When We First Met 29

Sadness 30

Vivid and Free 31

Funny Man 32

Winter Shadow 33

Pale October Morning 34

Starting Line 35

Cracker Girl 36

One 37

What Was I Thinking? 38

Plane 39

Determined 40

We fly together 41

Dedicated 42

Soundtrack 43

Age of Adolescence

The light opens to the world
and the day reacts to different situations
concerning the obstacles in front of you.
Decisions from right to wrong
fall down on your face,
while people judge, criticize and put you down
of the mistakes, in the part you choose to play in.
The wise one takes the best part
to smash you, to become nothing.
Laughter has the right to think highly,
but crying is a sorrow and pity to everyone else.
The searching of a very beautiful occasion
to love your parents as much as you did before.
Wishing that everything goes well with your plans
as they work unpredictably
with things happening unexpectedly.
Creating is a talent,
but disliking is a false,
when you're trying to look good
because you want to fit in like everyone else,
it's a law you just broke.
Leaving all your great and caring friends,
you thought they were a joke.
Causing trouble is not the start, trying to show off people
is the first job of hatred from your authentic self.

The fights and the blames result in breakups with a reminding of guiltiness.
Trying something new is the strength of the heart, trying less effect the weak body.
The craving for attention, you do anything to get it, the wanting for existence is hard enough.
Competition is dying to win, while crying turns to loss.
The sign of rejection gives you a low self-esteem.
Positivity wins it all.
Standing up for your rights is the conclusion of getting your needs.
Courage gives you an open space to try.
Patience in everyday life makes the story of your biography never run dry.

Like a Runaway
He sleeps less
stares at the ceiling
with a doubtful feeling.
Sounds quiet and peaceful,
maybe he's the first one to be awakening.
Strangers he once knew
used to communicate happily.
Now he crawls and hides somewhere
far away, just like a runaway.
Left empty, on his own.
Who to turn?
To his companions,
when they are home.
They say everything will get better,
but is that something to believe?
When he has all those hopes and dreams,
when will they ever come true?
Now he crawls and hides somewhere
far away, just like a runaway.
Everlasting nights, he wonders,
maybe there might be someone
out there tonight who can reach me?
He does not show the pain
he is going through.
No one can possibly understand.

Why was he so blind to see the real world?
He accepted it and followed everyone.
Still, he crawls and hides somewhere
far away, just like a runaway.

Attic
Feel the dryness around the room
surrounding old furniture
with wall cracks.
All the memories
are everywhere,
covered with dust
that was never been touched
nor cleaned.
The window is very unclear to see.
I slept here once
or was it a couple of times,
it wasn't scary
as I thought
it would be.

Waiting Game

Analyze the little objects that amaze you

Whine about the dumb things

that won't help you

get anywhere.
Stare at the light
when the sun
is shining on you.
Getting tense
when the day
isn't yet through.
The time doesn't want
to go quicker,
why is that?
I just can't stop
playing this waiting game.
Soon enough
I'll find my talent
of fears to blame.
Why would I want
to play this waiting game
if there is a road to take?
I'll show them when,
if only I'd finish

this journey of ours,
finding a shortcut
to get you there.
Why change to reality
when I'm safe where I am now,
while playing this waiting game?

Waiting for Liberty

Alone in the corner

with a feeling on my face,

too pink like a sunburn,
sitting uncomfortably
waiting for the bus
to arrive.
An old man
humming and talking
to himself
and others, surrounding
quietly and reading.
I, all by myself
just crushed.
I see the sunset
and the lights
starting to glow
in the dark.
I want to go, I really do,
but I don't have
that feeling
of independence

to push me through
what I want.
I wait with patience as is.
I'm falling in my conscience,
it's talking to me,
with the same voice I have.
"Go," it says.
"Do what your heart wants you to do."
Even though
when you are alone,
try to make it happen.
"You're letting yourself down."
Tears in my eyes start to show.

Describes You

I would like to stay here

as long as I want.

Sleep or eat,
it doesn't matter.
From my car rearview mirror,
I will see you.
When you are here or around,
you might see a glimpse of me
sitting in here,
staring at you gladly.
Here in my shelter,
I pretend not to wait for you.

One Summer Day

My hands are cold

as I slowly slide them into my pockets,

while walking in the stormy winter weather.
My feet are aching,
my hair through my scalp is numb, wet and tangled.
My hat won't help me keep my ears warm
and my coat's tight, it is giving me a very uncomfortable position to walk.
Let me think of one summer day with you
and wish all the snow could melt away.
I started to feel better when I arrived home.
I put my wet clothes aside.
Wore my nightgown, sat on the couch and watched a bit of TV,
while staring at the snowfall
from outside the window in front of me.
Let me think of one summer day with you
and wish all the snow could melt away.

Another Storm
Dark clouds appear,
ten minutes before it starts to pour.
A strong and powerful wind
bursts into flames.
The heavy weather
ruins the weak strength.
Rain starts to fall.
Everything calms down,
hearing only the sound
of a soft whistle of raindrops.
Everything changes
such as the beginning of a new day.

A Part of Reality

Never your journey will end

because of sweet faults block your way,
even though you weren't prepared for such greatness,
not believing such happiness addressed to you.
Take its worth of value,
that piece of gift that's called "Life."
Don't give it away, don't let sad rain pour on you
to diminish your existence.
Reach out to your soul and spirit,
you shouldn't care what they say.
Your freedom should be accepted
like life should be as is.

Why? I Think

I see you sitting on the grass
beside the willow tree, the park surrounding you.
Why? I think.
Don't you have better things to do?
Your strange looks marks of sadness, a sign of bad news.
Do I care about the loneliness you have?
I never see you in events that bring happiness in you.
Your dilemmas are erupting inside your body.
Why? I think.
People don't come close to you.
I wish I had some way to help.
I've heard you hum the music you listen to,
I've never heard such anger.
Why? I think.
You can't help yourself; maybe this is the way you are.
However, I don't see it in your eyes.

Wish

Bright moon
I share on my balcony, catch the stars as they fall.
I am never sober when you're not here with me.
These words of mine I cannot express to you,
because I'm telling this to someone who will make my future
bright as ever, like the galaxy above me.
I am scared to destroy it.
Have you ever had those moments that everything's all right?
Those are the moments when you are around.
I love to make you smile, it makes my days go wild.

My Heart is Bloomed

My conscience could tell if you're mine or not,
by just looking at the good times we had.
If I ask you one simple question, would you be able to answer it?
My heart is bloomed,
when you offer me plenty, my world starts to turn.
Do you ever think why we talk in different feelings every day?
I guess it's the way it should be.
Time goes by fast and I like it.
My heart is bloomed,
of the great sense when I'm always with you.
I can't believe what you said, what I thought in my heart right now.
What do you think?
I'll give you a few seconds, that great satisfaction around you,
is there with me forever.

Midsummer's Day

Swept up with a good feeling,

the face of beauty, in front of a new sunlight of the day.
The smell of sweet roses opens up to the light of life.
No signs of clouds, just happy rain that leaves moisture on the flowers petals.
That smile makes everything perfect; it falls from the sky.
Don't let go

You're Always There
These symptoms I have
describe each color of the rainbow.
The sunshine comes once in a while,
whatever happens,
you're always there.
I talk about anything, you understand clearly.
Morning, noon and night, days pass by
and you're always there.
The advices go on, vice-versa.
You're never lost, I can always find you,
because you're always there.

When We First Met
Hello, I said,
I hope this isn't the end,
with a smile I never showed to anyone, except you.
I changed my views of life to come close to my wanting,
the difficulty to find that special star.
I strain my eyes, they are weak and I give up.
My days are up to you.
Should I go on or think things through?

Sadness

My concentration of everyday life
holds me hostage like a prisoner,
whose life has to be in prison,
until the prisoner dies.
My expectations don't come wrapped with a nice ribbon on top,
they just stay there on the floor,
in front of my door.
Helplessly, I stand there looking
outside the window,
watching four seasons go by,
to find an answer that never had a question for it.
I suffer the pain for you,
but you don't know that, do you?
You're exactly like me,
loneliness is the power and the strength of every day.
The room full of dry air wins, sinking me in.
My health is low, anyone can take me over.

Vivid and Free

The need to stand on my own,
look around and watch the days go by.
Do not step on my path, it isn't necessary to find me.
I want to see clearly, like entering a new world.
Let my old news behind and no one comes to destroy my sight.
The time is ticking, I'm starting not to hold on,
reaching for my beginning line.

Funny Man
Whistles to the music in the near café,
hand gestures to the pretty ladies
as he looks for something to steal,
he walks and gives it to them
to be a nice man.

Winter Shadow

Smoky light spreads through me,
blinding every person with a weak power to go on.
Snow sheds on bodies, it stays there because of their cold skin.
Traffic circles into the mind with a rush for the change of routine,
of the winter shadow.
It covers us into a strong blur,
glory vanished with skeptical thoughts and grins with features through minds of people.
Damp dry air spinning in the house with a freezing breeze coming from the window,
where the winter shadow is.

Pale October Morning

Shivering, with a force of awakening,
there's no sun, I feel at ease.
Don't want to be bothered from the world.
The day, cold as ever,
even the water, too scared to touch.
No heat protects my existence from others
around.
The loud sounds erupt inside my head.
So much in dreams,
it doesn't feel
like I'm ever awake.
My day goes by,
like clocks when they're broken.

Starting Line
Soft or concrete
on a straight line.
Balance do not fall.
Color or black and white,
whichever you choose.

Cracker Girl

Bony, stiff and too pale,
you can see her veins very clearly.
I remember she was our subject at the cafeteria
table at school.
Sat alone in the corner with nothing to do,
just eat dull crackers.
Her eyes were small,
her hair was black, thin and short.
She had clothes without style,
she's cracker girl.
Different, quiet and weird.
We didn't want to ruin her off,
it's too cruel,
but she's cracker girl.

One
This isn't funny,
they are all bad lies,
trying to be treated fairly.
I know I care for you dearly.
Money's always the problem
we can't live without,
why people like us are always stuck in the big crowd?
We party when we can,
our minds are full of words,
what we learn is what we want to become.
But what I want is for us
to become one.

What Was I Thinking?
Pretty picture
that's what it seemed
it was hard to believe.
I knew that someday you would break the ice,
but all that steam in the air
covered your vision and made the truth so unclear.
Everything shattered,
like my heart did.
What joy did I see?
Suddenly you had to break the law,
without letting me know
so, I just had to let you go.
If this were to continue I would be in pain and wondering,
what would I gain?
You couldn't keep all your promises
and those silly words just fluttered around in the air.
Do you know how great you acted in the part of the play?
But in the last scene,
did you see yourself fall from the stage?
I did.

Plane
I lie awake on my bed,
my eyes are closed
as I hear a thunder passing by,
the sound of a plane
that had to fly.
It takes its direction to the nearest landing.
Sometimes I think, would it stop where I am?
So near,
so loud,
on the rooftop.
It feels so close,
as if I was at an airport,
but I am, it's where home is.

Determined
Soft sense of answers
makes me feel much better.
Organization of matter
holds my head up higher.
I have my own direction with a fear of happiness,
within me holds my strength of purity

We fly together
Would this be a good time to turn you into a butterfly?
With wings,
too colorful.
My heart should let you know
wherever I need to go
you have to follow.
The sun has set and I have just flown.

Dedicated

Is it wrong to look what should be craved for?
Very sweet,
its beauty that stands still…
What if I dream about that handsome angel?
It constructs my mind with delightful feelings.
Who knows?
Only you will show me the sign.

Soundtrack
The music of every song
takes you to a memory,
in another world,
where you once belonged.
The feelings you get in a closed place
where you walk,
trapped with thoughts
around the block.

www.ingramcontent.com/pod-product-compliance
Lightning Source LLC
Chambersburg PA
CBHW041125300426
44113CB00002B/58